Bicultural Identity Integration and Biculturalism of the Large-Scale Refugee Population Crisis: How Immigration, Assimilation, and Acculturation Changes and Influences Life

James Faber

July 19, 2016

This is a work of non-fiction and original academic research

ISBN 13: 978-1986848008
ISBN 10: 1986848000

Abstract

This article approaches the issue of immigration, integration, and assimilation from a bicultural perspective, and introduces applications of education, gender, and cultural awareness, as well as addressing and explaining the role of mass migration and how it could negatively effect and positively influence the economy. The specific goal of this article explores the issue of a large scale refugee population (mass migration) integrating, assimilating, and immigrating into a new country and culture. Immigrating, assimilating, or integrating might be hard for a refugee to do because the new culture is potentially different from what they already know and believe. This article examines how acculturation affects the overall immigration of the large-scale refugee population crisis. Currently, there is a refugee crisis around the world, due to the threat of terror and economic reasons. I predict that a multi-phase new bicultural approach (process), with an emphasis in education and or work, is the best way to combat the problem of why some refugees have issues immigrating, integrating, and assimilating into a new culture.

Keywords: Biculturalism, Large-Scale Refugee Population Crisis, Immigration, Assimilation, Acculturation

BICULTURAL IDENTITY INTEGRATION

Bicultural Identity Integration and Biculturalism of the Large-Scale Refugee Population Crisis: How Immigration, Assimilation, and Acculturation Changes and Influences Life

In today's society, many people feel they identify with more than one culture, simply because of their heritage and their beliefs. The emergence of an increase in globalization from countries around the world has made people to become increasingly multilingual and multicultural (Chen, Benet-Martínez, & Bond, 2008). The issue of being bicultural, or having two cultures, has been growing and is considered a social phenomenon (Nguyen & Benet-Martínez, 2013). As many as twenty-five percent out of all residents living in the United States of America have reported living in foreign countries before they moved or immigrated to the United States of America, and this could have internalized people to adopt more than one culture (Benet-Martínez & Haritatos, 2005). Some people might feel special and or confused because they are bicultural, and it could be due to the fact it is part of an identity issue (Benet-Martínez & Haritatos, 2005).

While language and culture can help shape the issue of being bilingual and bicultural, there can be priming effects (Chen, 2015). It can be stated that immigration and globalization has caused many consequences, and this has shifted more research concerning bilingualism and biculturalism being conducted (Chen, 2015). People who adopt an integration strategy towards biculturalism affirm not only their culture of origin but also of their new, second culture they will adopt (Chen et al., 2008). Yet, being bicultural and bilingual could be beneficial to a person, if they "do not internalize the conflict between the two intersecting cultures" (Chen, 2015, p. 1). This paper shall explore the issue of biculturalism and the theory of bicultural identity integration by Veronica Benet-Martínez, and how it relates of how large-scale refugee populations immigrate, assimilate, and experience acculturation in their new culture and society.

Analysis

History of Acculturation and Biculturalism

According to Nguyen and Benet-Martínez (2013), the process of adapting and learning a new and different culture is acculturation. Sociologists and anthropologists initiated and conducted past research regarding the issue of acculturation related to how society changes at a group level for migration (Chen et al, 2008). When psychologists studied the issue of (immigration-based) acculturation, they focused on how it impacted social changes, personal experiences, and psychological processes (Chen et al., 2008). As potential immigrants start to think about the process of cultural adaptation, research indicates that they could be classified into four different groups, based on how they feel about acculturation: assimilation, separation, integration, or marginalization (Chen et al., 2008).

In globalization-based acculturation, much of the research regarding bilingualism was conducted in the majority of western cultures, and specifically North America (Chen et al., 2008). Globalization could influence psychological functioning, causing an impact to identity issues, thus it could be considered consequential (Chen et al., 2008). Traditional bicultural identities might not be the most important issue regarding globalization-based acculturation, but instead would be about how cultural elements are selectively incorporated from the numerous practices and worldviews a person has been exposed to (Chen et al., 2008). In the United States of America, the theory of biculturalism and bicultural identity could be referred as a melting pot, because larger urban centers became culturally pluralist (de Anda, 1984).

To explain biculturalism in America, a six-factor model could be utilized, as well as the cultural deficit model and the cultural difference model (de Anda, 1984). The cultural deficit model was important during the war on poverty, and posited that minority groups' cultural patterns and norms were destructive and deviant that it caused a cycle of deprivation and poverty (de Anda, 1984). From this conceptualization, the cultural deficit model was discredited and useless, and resulted in the cultural difference model (de Anda, 1984). Instead of focusing on poverty and deprivation, the cultural difference model focused on how each minority culture was unique and could be considered independent, yet it received criticism because it could not explain how members of minority groups could socially integrate within the majority group (de Anda, 1984).

From this cultural difference model, a bicultural model was proposed, and it explained that anyone from an ethnic minority group could belong to two behavioral repertoires, one for the minority group and the other for the majority group (de Anda, 1984). Yet, the bicultural model does not fully explain how successful ethnic minorities and other people within the ethnic minorities when success related to the majority society was never based on the process of assimilation (de Anda, 1984). In Valentine's concept of biculturalism, he believed each culture was distinct and separate, but it is possible because dual socialization is facilitated by the amount of overlap between both cultures (de Anda, 1984).

To put the biculturalism model into perspective, European immigrants were successful according to the melting pot theory, because of their vast area of similar norms and shared values (de Anda, 1984). Yet, for Afro-Americans, Hispanics, and Asian immigrants, the melting pot theory was not applicable to them, possibly because of conflicting views (de Anda, 1984). From this, the bicultural model explained maturity and responsibility were viewed differently in Hispanic cultures than the mainstream Caucasian culture (de Anda, 1984). Research indicated that immigrants and ethnic minorities who acculturate have to deal with two main issues: the motivation or permission to keep their culture of origin identity and if they are motivated or need permission to join their new dominant culture (Benet-Martínez & Haritatos, 2005). Nevertheless, some researchers see acculturation as a non-linear process, but instead believe it is a multidimensional process that seeks to describe an immigrant can belong to their ethnic culture as well as to the larger society (Benet-Martínez & Haritatos, 2005).

Current research indicates that the new multidimensional and bidirectional approach towards acculturation is superior to many unidimensional models in predicting outcomes, because of psychometric validity (Benet-Martínez & Haritatos, 2005). Recently, cultural frame switching, the shifting between the cultural orientations, was posited, by how bicultural people moved between their two cultures, as how they could maintain both of their cultures (Benet-Martínez & Haritatos, 2005). The majority of traditional acculturation research studies has posited that biculturalism was a uniform construct, failing to consider any individual variations in how can be organized and negotiated (Benet-Martínez & Haritatos, 2005).

From this finding, the traditional and custom acculturation scales are said to be deficient, because they fail to capture the fundamental individual differences of how experiences and meanings can be affiliated with bicultural identity (Benet-Martínez & Haritatos, 2005). As a result, to fill the gaps in present and prior research regarding acculturation and biculturalism, Benet-Martínez and her colleagues proposed the bicultural identity integration as a theoretical construct to be the framework to investigate any individual differences in the organization of bicultural identity (Benet-Martínez & Haritatos, 2005). This new theoretical construct focused on how bicultural people's subjective perceptions of their percentage of dual cultural identities can intersect and or overlap (Benet-Martínez & Haritatos, 2005). Since Benet-Martínez wanted to propose a new theoretical construct and framework to identify individual differences in bicultural identity, it could be viewed as biased, because she only wants to know about certain gaps within individuals (Benet-Martínez & Haritatos, 2005). Although, it could also be seen as biased because it groups low scorers of bicultural identity integration into difficulty of integrating both cultures in a case of identity, there could other reasons why this occurs, such as an immigrant feeling homesick (Benet-Martínez & Haritatos, 2005).

Theorist Background

The theorist who proposed the Bicultural Identity Integration Theory, Veronica Benet-Martínez, graduated with a baccalaureate in psychology at the Autonomous University of Barcelona in Spain (Benet-Martínez, Lee, & Leu, 2006). Following her undergraduate education, Benet-Martínez pursued a doctorate in social personality at the University of California Davis, and then became a postdoctoral researcher at the University of California at Berkeley (Benet-Martínez, Lee, & Leu, 2006). The theorist was a faculty member of the University of Michigan until 2003, and then moved back to California to become a faculty member at the University of California at Riverside (Benet-Martínez, Lee, & Leu, 2006). At the University of California Riverside, Benet-Martínez started the culture and personality laboratory (Benet-Martínez, Lee, & Leu, 2006).

Currently, Benet-Martínez is a professor at the Catalan Institute for Research and Advanced Studies, as well as a professor at Pampeu Fabra University in Spain (Benet-Martínez, 2016). In 2016, Benet-Martínez was a visiting fellow at the City University of New York graduate center, focusing on immigration (Benet-Martínez, 2016). Throughout her career, Benet-Martínez focused on the fields of multi/bicultural identity, culture and personality, and cross-cultural research methods (Benet-Martínez, 2016). Benet-Martínez (2016) approaches her research investigations by using experimental, longitudinal, and correlational research designs. As she is primarily interested in culture, Benet-Martínez (2016) wants to know how biculturalism affects the cognitive, social, and adjustment constructs of a person, yet she also wants to know any personal differences in the structure of a person's bicultural identity.

Characteristics and Methods

As described above, Benet-Martínez (2016) uses many methods to conduct her research. Bicultural identity integration seeks to determine how much of a person's dual cultural identities either overlap or intersect (Benet-Martínez & Haritatos, 2005). The basis of bicultural identity integration was from an extensive review relating to literature regarding empirical and qualitative acculturation as well as biculturalism (Benet-Martínez & Haritatos, 2005). Previous acculturation studies indicated biculturalism as a uniform construct

BICULTURAL IDENTITY INTEGRATION

(Benet-Martínez & Haritatos, 2005). The goal of bicultural identity integration is to determine how "biculturals perceive their mainstream and ethnic cultural identities as compatible and integrated vs. oppositional and difficult to integrate" (Benet-Martínez & Haritatos, 2005, p. 1019). The research identified variations of sociocultural, socioeconomical, and sociocognitive factors in the formation of bicultural identity (Benet-Martínez & Haritatos, 2005).

The measure proposed by Benet-Martínez and her colleagues was named the BIIS-1, also known as the bicultural identity integration scale (version 1), and this was supposed to be better than previous bicultural scales because it included the key constructs of cultural distance and cultural conflict (Benet-Martínez & Haritatos, 2005; Miramontez, Benet-Martínez, & Nguyen, 2008). Instead of being perceived as having two latent dimensional constructs of cultural distance and cultural conflict, bicultural identity integration should be seen as an emergence or results of variations in those two key psychological constructs (Benet-Martínez & Haritatos, 2005). It was also found that the two psychological constructs of cultural distance and cultural conflict were associated with numerous sets of antecedents relating to acculturation and disposition (Benet-Martínez & Haritatos, 2005).

Within these two constructs, there are specific attitudes, behaviors, and feelings relating to their overall nature, as to how it relates to a person (Benet-Martínez & Haritatos, 2005). The cultural distance portion of the scale involves how a bicultural person perceives their cultural identities as either fused and or hyphenated or being disassociated (Miramontez et al., 2008). In the cultural conflict portion of the scale, the bicultural person might be described as being conflicted or confused about their two cultural identities (Miramontez et al., 2008). Bicultural people who experience cultural conflict tend to have a form of neuroticism and have a form of stress in the intercultural relations, linguistic, and discrimination domains, and this could possibly challenge feelings relating to efficacy, causing inconsistencies in harmonious self-images (Benet-Martínez & Haritatos, 2005).

From the conflict of inconsistencies within self-images of cultural conflicts, it is the reason why some bicultural individuals have had trouble deciding which culture to belong to (Benet-Martínez & Haritatos, 2005). Aside from cultural conflict, there is also cultural distance, which can be connected or related to the construct of alternation (Benet-Martínez & Haritatos, 2005). Bicultural individuals who experience high cultural distance could keep their ethnic and new culture (American) separate from each other (Benet-Martínez & Haritatos, 2005). Bicultural individuals who experience cultural distance might have low openness, as well as stress in the linguistic setting and in how someone experiences cultural isolation (Benet-Martínez & Haritatos, 2005). From the factors within the concept of cultural distance, it could be said that biculturalism could be seen as a dichotomy (Benet-Martínez & Haritatos, 2005). From these two constructs of cultural distance and cultural conflict, there is the concept of cultural frame switching, which is the process of bicultural individuals moving between their two cultural orientations (Benet-Martínez & Haritatos, 2005).

The process of cultural frame switching involves bicultural individuals moving or shifting between their two cultural identities due to cultural cues from the environment (Miramontez et al., 2008). To approach cultural frame switching, it is possible to use social psychology ideas relating to dual group identity (Verkuyten & Pouliasi, 2006). It is possible for a bicultural individual to have more than one cultural frame, even if there are conflicting elements, yet they do not guide simultaneous thinking (Verkuyten & Pouliasi, 2006). However, biculturalism and cultural frame switching should not be restricted just towards cognitive mechanisms, but should also be applied to intergroup scenarios (Verkuyten & Pouliasi, 2006). It is applicable to indicate that bicultural identity integration should be applied to future research, since it was recently proposed, and it is reasonable to measure cultural conflict and cultural distance in order to solve any potential problems (Cheng, Lee, & Benet-Martínez, 2006; Benet-Martínez & Haritatos, 2005).

Regardless of the growth and development of the bicultural identity integration scale, because it is still in its infancy, since it was proposed in 2002 (Benet-Martínez & Haritatos, 2005). Although, the research relating to biculturalism was related to Chinese-American studies, the theory has been applied towards other populations, such as Greek adolescents residing in the Netherlands, as well as Latinos living in the United States of America (Benet-Martínez & Haritatos, 2005; Verkuyten & Pouliasi, 2002; Miramontez et al., 2008). Even though it is still in its early stages, the bicultural identity integration theory should be applied towards other concepts, such as that of self-concept, the personal construct system, and how it relates to social learning and social interaction.

Evaluation

Validity and Accuracy

Biculturalism has been increasing in many countries and is constantly growing, so to understand the situation better Benet-

Martínez and her colleagues wanted to find alternate ways in how bicultural identities are handled (Smith, Fischer, Vignoles, & Bond, 2013). Bicultural identity integration has shown to have good predictive validity, as it was applied to many other cultural environments, while the measures have also improved (Smith et al., 2013). Bicultural identity integration has the capability of understanding acculturation better and can provide for the possibility of how acculturation can be successful in migrants (Smith et al., 2013). From this, it could be said that bicultural individuals could identify with their self-concept and their personal constructs, and psychologists could attempt to use those characteristics to better understand how bicultural individuals interact within their ethnic culture as well as their new majority culture.

The self-concept by Carl Rogers is a representation of organization of consistencies in patterns of perceptions (Cervone & Pervin, 2016). Rogers identified two concepts of the self: the actual self and the ideal self, in which the ideal self would be the aspect of self-concept that a person would want to possess (Cervone & Pervin, 2016). In the aspect of the ideal self, it could be seen as the potential of perceptions and meanings that could describe relevancy and could be highly valuable for the individual (Cervone & Pervin, 2016). In bicultural individuals, the ideal self could be seen as a way to help guide them towards the necessary goals to help them better acculturate into their new majority culture, as well as keeping their current ethnic culture. There is also the concept of self-actualization, which involves life being an active process and that it must be maintained, actualized, and enhanced in order to strive and live (Cervone & Pervin, 2016). Bicultural individuals could use this process of actualization to better understand what they need to do in order to survive into their new majority culture, and by taking the considerations from self-actualization into context, it is possible they will better acculturate (Cervone & Pervin, 2016).

Thereby, it could be stated that bicultural individuals who can assimilate their experiences into their self-structure are better and healthier, resulting in better acculturation into their new majority culture (Cervone & Pervin, 2016). Yet, the Big Five model could explain acculturation and biculturalism better, due to it being a factor-analytic approach (Cervone & Pervin, 2016). Instead of building personality on numerous variables, the big five theories support an adoption of natural language, otherwise known as words to describe personality (Cervone & Pervin, 2016). Bicultural individuals might use these individual words to describe how they fit into their new majority culture, and how they would feel about acculturation. At the same time, international researchers could have made cross-cultural research better, because they have found universal traits (Cervone & Pervin, 2016).

By explaining that the Big Five Theory can be universal across cultures, psychologists could better understand that bicultural individuals having trouble assimilating or acculturating into their new majority culture might display some of the same traits. In fact, a version of the big five personality inventory was used to assess the prototypical traits in individuals in line with the big five model, and it was found to have excellent reliability and validity in studies relating to European-Americans and individuals belonging to the ethnic minorities (Benet-Martínez & Haritatos, 2005). In explaining the big five theory, low extraversion could predict a bicultural individual is experiencing cultural isolation, yet it was explained that the model could be associated to psychosocial outcomes, yet not much research connecting this to the acculturation process (Benet-Martínez & Haritatos, 2005). With regard how the big five model represents descriptors, the personal construct system posited by George Kelly believes that everything is related to a series of constructs or elements of knowledge (Cervone & Pervin, 2016).

The personal construct system involves a theory of cognition (Cervone & Pervin, 2016). Based on constructive alternativism, a bicultural individual could use alternate constructs to better understand and view a different, more useful perspective of the world (Cervone & Pervin, 2016). Based on this, if a bicultural individual is having problems acculturating or assimilating into their new majority culture, then they can attempt to look into a different direction into how they can acculturate better. Psychologists could also use this construct of alternativism to determine how to approach of acculturation better by exploring how bicultural individuals have problems with adapting to their new culture.

In the prospect of the construct model, it could be stated that personality in regards to bicultural identity could have cognitive complexity (Cheng, Lee, Benet-Martínez, & Huynh, 2014). High cognitive complexity could mean a bicultural individual has blended bicultural identity, and often demonstrate more creativity (Cheng et al., 2014). Yet, motivation could describe why biculturals could have potential problems adapting to new cultures and norms within their new majority culture, but it all goes back to the concept of understanding social cues within the environment (Cheng et al., 2014). From a more specific perspective, it would be better to understand biculturalism from the main two different types of cultures, in order to provide a better analysis of contemporary relevancy, yet bicultural individuals attempt to internalize both of their belief systems from their two cultures they have resided in (Cervone & Pervin, 2016).

Contemporary Relevance

From the perspective of culture, there are two main types of cultures: individualistic and collectivist (Cohen, Swerdlik, & Sturman, 2013). In an individualistic culture a bicultural person might attempt to deal with their own problems because everything is about promoting one's own beliefs and ideology (Cohen et al., 2013). However, in a collectivist culture, a bicultural individual might not be able to express their own opinions because the ideology promotes a larger group, such as the family (Cohen et al., 2013). In both cultures, a bicultural individual could face problems adapting to new cultures, because of problems within both beliefs systems, and these problems could cause the reason why they fail to adapt to their new cultures.

It is important for people to understand that different cultures should be taken into perspective when discussing the issue about acculturation and biculturalism. Bicultural identity integration is important in today's society of biculturalism, acculturation, and assimilation; because it can provide for a better understanding of how bicultural people cope or adjust with their two cultures. In the concept of psychological adjustment, it can include the aspects of life satisfaction, self-esteem, depression, alienation, and anxiety (Nguyen & Benet-Martínez, 2013). In the concept of sociocultural adjustment, it can entail career success, achievements in education, and social skills (Nguyen & Benet-Martínez, 2013). Yet, there could be adjustment relating to health issues, which can include low amounts of somatic symptoms and high amounts of eating healthy as well as high levels of physical activity (Nguyen & Benet-Martínez, 2013).

Even more, biculturalism related to acculturation strategies could help bicultural individuals to better adjust to life (Nguyen & Benet-Martínez, 2013). At the same time, it could be stated that biculturals could be better adjusted to their culture and society because of their competency navigating their dominant (majority culture) and their heritage culture, also known as their ethnic culture (Nguyen & Benet-Martínez, 2013). In another relevant aspect of today's society, bicultural individuals often are bilingual, yet linguists have explored the issue of bilingualism (Chen, 2015). In order to understand biculturalism better, it is important to understand the concepts of bilingualism and identity, since it is part by being psychological healthy, because it could better explain integration, attitudes, and any other possible barriers (Chen, 2015). It could also be stated that leaving the family home is relevant in modern society towards the issue of biculturalism and acculturation because of how someone wants to become independent (Lou, Lalonde, & Giguère, 2012).

From the idea of moving out, there is the possibility of moving on, and this could mean migrating from eastern to western countries (Lou et al., 2012). Migration, immigration, or seeking asylum is largely relevant in modern society regarding the issue of biculturalism, since it relates to how a person could choose to become bicultural because they want to experience a new transition in life (Lou et al., 2012). From that notion, it is important to understand that biculturals or people who choose to become bicultural by migration (becoming immigrants and or refugees), will face many challenges in life, because there is a factor of socialization, family, and culture, relating to influence (Lou et al., 2012).

Multiphase Approach to Issue

Problem

The problem regarding a complex issue within the concepts of biculturalism, acculturation, and bicultural identity integration is the issue of mass migration by refugees, also known as the large-scale mass refugee problem that is currently happening around the world. To put it into further context, many migrants of this large-scale refugee crisis are having problems assimilating within their new majority cultures, and they fail to accept their new surroundings, and sometimes they are unable to control their impulses, due to their original ethnic culture. It is evident that bicultural individuals with low bicultural identity integration have many more negative cultural associations while bicultural individuals with higher amounts of bicultural identity integration experience less acculturation stress, indicating it could represent an asset (Cheng et al., 2006).

Moreover, bicultural individuals (immigrants and refugees) with high bicultural identity integration have a more secure sense of the self than that of those with lower bicultural identity integration (Mok & Morris, 2009). The reason for the difference in responding to cultural cues regarding assimilation could be due to internal identity management (Mok & Morris, 2009). Nevertheless, the issue of mass migration with regard to immigrants and refugees not assimilating and acculturating properly, is an increasing problem and it needs to be solved properly, not just a one-sized-fits-all model that is flawed. Instead, to approach the issue of mass migration regarding immigrants and refugees not assimilating and acculturating properly, each case needs to be vetted individually, and strict new protocols need to be adopted to make the crisis decrease.

Solution

The solution that I propose to the mass migration issue regarding immigrants and refugees not assimilating and acculturating properly is a multi-step bicultural approach with an emphasis in education and or work, however, I will describe first why current migration policies fail to work. From this perspective of the failed migration policies, I will describe many points and guidelines that hope to make the current system anywhere flawless or almost flawless. By having a multiphase approach, it is possible to reduce an abuse of the system, and this will provide an incentive for border security as well as national security (both domestically and internationally). Current migration policies regarding immigration and refugees fail because of the social dynamics regarding the migration process, the divide between the North and the South due to globalization, and politics (Castles, 2004). Within all factors, there are certain key issues that might make migration policies fail, issues such as certain harbored beliefs (Castles, 2004).

Such beliefs within the factors regarding migration and social dynamics can be due to cost-benefit calculations and bureaucratic regulations (Castles, 2004). Yet, those two beliefs fail to recognize the concept of historical experiences, because guest workers who sought temporary residency were thought to move back to their previous culture, but they actually decided to live there permanently (Castles, 2004). Within the factor of the North-South divide, there is a reason migration can fail, because of gross inequality and uneven development (Castles, 2004). Additionally, globalization creates strong cultural pressures regarding mobilization of migration, yet many governments fail to notice the importance of unskilled workers, and this lack of knowledge does make it possible why immigrants decide to cross borders illegally (Castles, 2004).

Nevertheless, the policies are simply too complex, with too many contradictions relating to economics and social interests (Castles, 2004). Inclusion could be a factor why current migration policies fail, yet, it could be better for countries to take a more simple approach that would ease current controls (Castles, 2004). However, regardless of the current solutions offered, I believe they are seriously flawed because they fail to underestimate the current crisis. Instead of focusing on what could happen, the central and national governments of the European Union are employing migration policies that fail to detect the current crisis at hand, the fact that mass migration is occurring because of global events, and that they are focusing more on illegal immigration and less on how to prevent a crisis, thus making it too complex (Castles, 2004).

Proposed Solution

My proposed solution to the issue regarding mass migration and why immigrants and refugees not assimilating and acculturating properly is a seven-point (multiphase) plan that seeks to solve the actual problem better, with less complexity and something that makes more sense. Although, some people might say it is complex because of the multiple steps, I see it as important to control migration in a much simpler, less restrictive manner. In this way, the plan should help the current residents and citizens of the countries, as well as the borders, and the safety of the countries and the governments.

My multiphase approach to the problem is as follows:

BICULTURAL IDENTITY INTEGRATION

1. Institute a recognition and identification system: This first phase will determine if the migrants seeking a new home are actually not a threat to their homeland as well as to their new country and culture. Governments and their agencies will have the potential to communicate with each other.

2. Study current migration laws concerning eligibility of acceptance: This second phase will allow the governments to study their migration and asylum laws. If anything is too complex or if it is too lenient, then there is a potential problem.

3. Institute Border control conditions: After studying the laws, implement a border control system that is not too restrictive but not too lenient. This means that not every potential migrant will be accepted immediately (condition status), but they could be put onto a waiting list while being vetted (probationary status).

4. Education: Non-migrants (citizens and residents) and potential migrants can learn how to deal with mass migration and what might be necessary to take place. There would be seminars available, but migrants could enroll in language classes and seminars, and they could enroll their children into the school systems, and they would be able to learn how to integrate better to their new culture by learning the necessary tools to survive.

5. Test the program: This should be offered on a case-by-case basis for a few months, up to a year, to see if there are any complications regarding assimilation and acculturation. The government should offer any migrant, with either conditional or probationary status, the opportunity to live and work in their new culture. The migrants will be tracked to see if they follow the law and are faithful to their new environment.

6. Reevaluation: The entire program should be reevaluated after one year to three years (if applicable). After reevaluating, determine if there are any major issues, but there should not be any issues if it was instituted correctly.

7. Implementation: Implement the entire program by making it available to all immigrants and refugees. However, if any migrants (immigrants or refugees) have trouble with the law, acculturating, and assimilating, then consider deportation proceedings for those particular individuals.

With my multiphase approach, it is possible to institute a less complex migration policy, as well as something that could actually work. However, everything needs to be gradual, but if it is not, then it could potentially fail, because quick solutions do not exist and are incapable of working (Messner, 2015). At the same time, it is important to consider protecting the new immigrants or refugees, because they are going through a difficult process of adapting to a new culture (Messner, 2015). It is important to review everything, as refugee and immigration policies tend to be outdated, and needs to be conducted to better suit humanity (Messner, 2015). Without education, there would be much confusion about what is happening, but a bad immigration and refugee policy will also make it worse (Messner, 2015).

Immigration has to be largely based on acculturation, assimilation, and biculturalism, because it is all about adapting to a new society and culture. In fact, immigration is largely based on these issues, but the problems lies within the more severe problem of mass migration policies. Research indicated that immigration control did change, but I believe it is constantly changing, and needs to change, in order to catch up, because at the current situation, there is no solution that is effective enough at working (Schain, 2009). Patterns of immigration are changing, but state control could interfere with the process, but international agreements could have caused more harm because of a one-size-fits-all model has been adopted (Schain, 2009). With my approach, there would be no one-size-fits-all model, because every immigrant will be treated on a case-by-case basis.

The Need for Better Education

Even more, liberal democracies, such as those in Europe, have trouble instituting reform, because of national and international constraints, yet the court systems still do interfere, and even they can cause problems (Schain, 2009). In my approach, the immigrants or refugees will only face the court system, if they break the law or are not acculturating, assimilating, and integrating properly. Successful immigrants and refugees would need access to everything that the current residents and the citizens have to integrate better towards their new culture, because it provides a framework to see if they will adapt (Schain, 2009). There has been a significant shift in attitudes of politicians regarding the issue of mass migration, because of a political and economic crisis (Lesińska, 2014). Often, legal immigration gets blamed because of illegal immigrants, but it could also be due to the problem that some people want to commit crimes (Lesińska, 2014).

Nevertheless, the general population is often critical of certain religions and cultures, because of what has been currently happening around the world (Lesińska, 2014). Currently, they have an opinion about one culture and religion because they see it happening every day and view it as a crisis, yet they also take it out on that religion because they believe everything is the same about everyone who believes in that religion and culture, thus it becomes a sentiment of fear (Lesińska,

2014). Politicians have been using propaganda to attack certain ethnic minorities, because they believe they can control the borders and migration borders better, but often, they tend to see it as inefficient (Lesińska, 2014). Multiculturalism is often targeted, and it is often attacked, because of being inefficient, but some ethnic minorities could have problems acculturating, integrating, and assimilating into their new culture, because they just do not want to adapt (Lesińska, 2014).

Addressing the Solution

Assessment and Defense

Furthermore, my approach to the mass migration issue does include a language requirement as well as a citizenship requirement, if the immigrants and refugees want to become citizens, but it is the same regulation and procedure for potential migrants who want to live and work in Europe (Lesińska, 2014). Yet, immigration reform in the United States of America was largely a choice of civil rights, in order to improve human conditions and people decided to take on the Vietnam War, as well as taking part in riots (Massey & Pren, 2012). From another account, illegal immigration increased after 1965 from Mexico due to the termination of a special visa-working program (Massey & Pren, 2012). Implementing a program within my approach would probably provide for less illegal immigration and better acculturation, assimilation, and integration, because the immigrants and refugees can work in their new culture while they are waiting to be vetted.

Even more, immigration reform in the United States of America has been complex to grapple, because Americans can experience anxiety regarding what the new immigrants or refugees will do, but there is often a political aspect (Weir, 2011). Some presidents did try to tackle the issue, but it has often been a process of comprehensive review, but they did seek massive reform, but there was always political pressure (Weir, 2011). An incremental approach is a good start to implement in order to reform immigration policy, and my approach to the problem can be incremental because it is gradual (Weir, 2011). From a more practical matter, my solution and approach to the problem can be considered very comprehensive, because it involves many necessary steps required for successful integration, assimilation, and acculturation in a new culture.

Mass Migration Explained. Mass migration is another term for the large-scale refugee problem. It has the same context, and often involves immigrants and refugees migrating to a new country that contains a new culture and society. With regard to mass migration, and the problem at hand, why a large group of immigrants and refugees fail to assimilate, acculturate, and integrate into their new culture, is that because there could be a clash of cultures (Messner, 2015; Lou et al., 2012). By definition, mass migration often involves a vast amount of people moving from one geographical location to another (Pok, 2012). Mass migration is usually caused by a series of events, such as terrorism or economic instability, and can last for many years until the threat stops (Pok, 2012).

Often, large-scale seasonal migration exists, happening periodically and with repetitions, but that is different, due to people looking for a temporary job and then returning to their home (Pok, 2012). Yet, the difference with mass migration is that it often proceeds into permanent settlement (Pok, 2012). It is important to differentiate between mass migration and seasonal migration, because both of them involve the process of migrating to a new location, but one is temporary while the other could be permanent (Pok, 2012). Nevertheless, with mass migration, there is the possibility of many problems occurring, such as social burdens and the issue relating to economics, but migration can often be seen as something good, because it can decrease the working age, which can potentially help increase the working economy (Weede, 2015). Yet, increasing the working economy is only a part of the issue.

    Economic Issues and Burdens. Mass migration, or any aspect of migration, can benefit and harm society. In one manner, migration and even mass migration can help the economy because it can increase the workforce drastically, while younger immigrants and refugees have a better education then the previous generations seeking retirement (Organisation for Economic Co-operation and Development [OECD], 2014). It was stated that there is no social burden from immigrants or refugees, because they pay more taxes and endow more social contributions, but also receive less benefits (OECD, 2014). However, while migrants have many skills and can benefit society by helping the economy, there are possible consequences, such as costs (Bonin, Rowan, & Zimmermann, 2008; OECD, 2014). Nevertheless, the costs could potentially outweigh the benefits, because the factors of social tensions and divisions are not easy to assess (Bonin et al., 2008).

    Even more, there is a problem of who will cover these economic costs, and this also includes any fiscal costs relating to the current immigration policies (Bonin et al., 2008). If the immigrants and refugees are selected based upon the basis for helping them integrate into society and to be placed into the labor market, then it is possible that "language training and other integration costs will not be as high as when a large proportion of immigrants come under family reunion or humanitarian criteria" (Bonin et al., 2008, p. 150). Yet, different nations have a different approach to integration: some have integration policies that are mandated while others have no such program (Bonin et al., 2008). In some instances, businesses might have an important role in migration and integration programs, yet it is important to understand the immigration policies and programs of each country (Bonin et al., 2008). Governments can attract immigrants and refugees by introducing welfare and tax programs, but there also could be a burden of cultural heterogeneity (Weede, 2015).

Moreover, when mass migration exists, there can be an increase in cultural heterogeneity (Weede, 2015). Indeed, the welfare sectors can have a negative influence on migration, leading to the reason why many politicians and people do not support increasing the threshold of accepting more refugees or immigrants (Ruist, 2015). Nevertheless, it could be stated that an open door policy of accepting immigrants and refugees and an attractive welfare state can decrease the prospects for the future (Weede, 2015). However, the cause for this concern could be due to refugees having very low employment rates, as well as very high use of benefits, making refugees less attractive (Ruist, 2015). From any perspective, it could be stated there could be social burdens and economic problems for accepting mass migration, but there are also reasons that these same problems could support the refugees if the programs and policies are adopted in an excellent and appropriate manner.

Education and Cultural Awareness. In retrospect, an excellent immigration and refugee policy should always include education, because it will provide the necessary tools to survive. Schools and other educational institutions are important to potential immigrants and refugees because it can help them better integrate into society. For example, the children and adolescents of immigrants and refugees could be enrolled in English courses utilizing ESOL. English for Speakers of Other Languages (ESOL) is a largely used tactic in school systems, in order for the student to better understand the language, in order to learn the language. ESOL is most likely conducted using special software like Rosetta Stone, utilizing an immersion technique that allows for the user to learn as they go. By understanding their new language, the student would be able to integrate better into society, potentially understanding the norms and standards better, and they will have a better chance to assimilate and acculturate.

As a result of education, it is important to understand that seminars can be held in order to explain cultural awareness, and this could occur because people can feel threatened if they do not know about the true nature of the culture they are afraid of. There have been many cultural shifts, and they will continue to occur, because everything is always changing. Yet, recent news indicates that later generations are having trouble assimilating into society, but their parents have no problem at all. But, parents could also face bicultural identity issues, such as bicultural management difficulty (Kim, Shen, Huang, Wang, & Orozco-Lapray, 2014). Chinese-American parents might find it difficult to manage their bicultural identity, because they might want to act more Chinese and sometimes more American, and this could be due to a lack of confidence or even a lack of comfortability (Kim et al., 2014). However, this could be due to depressive symptoms, but it is also a possibility that not all immigrants and refugees want to assimilate, integrate, or acculturate into society (Kim et al., 2014).

Gender and Culture. To relate gender and culture into bicultural situations, it is important to understand that there is a different belief system. For instance, China is a collectivist culture, and family is the most important aspect of life, but in America, people value freedom and liberty (Benet-Martínez, Lee, & Leu, 2006). In China, the eldest male is groomed to be the heir of the family, and is supposed to take care of everything, while any female sibling is only a temporary member of their original family, but devotes time to her husband's extended family once married (Xie, 2013). China has largely gender inequality, but that is not just unique to their culture, however, it is important to note that bicultural identity integration within Chinese immigrants or refugees is excellent, as they have no problem learning their new culture (Xie, 2013; Chen, 2015).

It is important to understand that not all cultures are supportive of all people, but that might be due to the consequence of globalization and immigration (Chen, 2015). It could be psychologically stressful for immigrants and refugees to experience biculturalism and bilingualism (Chen, 2015). As more people internalize more than one culture, there tends to be an increase every year (Verkuyten & Pouliasi, 2006). Nevertheless, it is vital to understand that biculturalism can cause many psychological questions to be asked, because it is important for potential biculturals to shift between their ethnic culture and their new dominant culture (Verkuyten & Pouliasi, 2006).

Conclusion

In summary, I believe bicultural identity integration is an important aspect and tool of learning how to acculturate, assimilate, and integrate better into a new culture. As technology is increasing, so is intercultural contact and interactions (Nguyen, 2013). Immigration and refugee policies are largely outdated, and they need to be addressed and fixed. Mass migration is an increasingly important problem, but as people demand change, there is an issue of whether if the new refugees or immigrants will actually acculturate, assimilate, and integrate into their new culture. From my solution to the mass migration issue, I believe it is multi-faceted, but I also favor an emphasis in education in order to improve the chances of successful acculturation, assimilation, and integration.

Overall, bicultural identity integration is a good way to start helping immigrants and refugees to better assimilate into new cultures. My approach allows for immigrants and refugees to receive either conditional or probationary status, and during that grace period while being vetted they can work, and it could indicate if they are integrating properly into their new culture. Biculturalism and acculturation is important to address, and without a good policy, there would not be good integration. For any reason, immigration needs to be fixed, because it is causing chaos around the world, while governments still implement poor policies that do not work. For any reason, while mass migration of refugees and immigrants can be seen as good for the economy and the country, it can also be seen as unattractive, because of what the refugees and immigrants actually contribute to their new country (OECD, 2014; Ruist, 2015).

References

Benet-Martínez, V. (2016). Curriculum Vitae. Retrieved from
https://www.icrea.cat/Web/ScientificStaff/veronica-benet-
martinez-518.

Benet-Martínez, V., & Haritatos, J. (2005). Bicultural identity
integration (BII): Components and psychosocial antecedents.
Journal of Personality 73(4), 1015-1050, doi: 10.1111/j.1467-
6494.2005.00337.x.

Benet-Martínez, V., Lee, F., & Leu, J. (2006). Biculturalism and
cognitive complexity: Expertise in cultural representations.
Journal of Cross-Cultural Psychology, 37(4), 386-407, doi:
10.1177/0022022106288476.

Bonin, H., Rowan, R., & Zimmermann, K.F. (2008). Comparing and
evaluating public expenditure on migration. In S. Ardittis & F.
Laczko (Eds.), *Assessing the costs and impacts of migration
policy: An international comparison* (137-190). Geneva,
Switzerland: International Organization for Migration.

Castles, S. (2004). Why migration policies fail. *Ethnic and Racial
Studies, 27*(2), 205-227, doi: 10.1080/0141987042000177306.

Cervone, D., & Pervin, L.A. (2016). *Personality: Theory and research*
(13th ed.). Hoboken, NJ: John Wiley and Sons.

Chen, S.X., Benet-Martínez, V., & Bond, M.H. (2008). Bicultural
identity, bilingualism, and psychological adjustment in
multicultural societies: Immigration-based and globalization-
based acculturation. *Journal of Personality, 76*(4), 803-838,
doi: 10.1111/j.1467-6494.2008.00505.x.

Chen, S.X. (2015). Toward a social psychology of bilingualism and biculturalism. *Asian Journal of Social Psychology, 18*, 1-11, doi: 10.1111/ajsp.12088.

Cheng, C.Y., Lee, F., Benet-Martínez, V., & Huynh, Q.L. (2014). Variations in multicultural experience: Influence of bicultural identity integration on socio-cognitive processes and outcomes. *The Oxford Handbook of Multicultural Identity*, 1-28, doi: 10.1093/oxfordhb/9780199796694.013.025.

Cheng, C.Y., Lee, F., & Benet-Martínez, V. (2006). Assimilation and contrast effects in cultural frame switching: Bicultural identity integration and valence of cultural cues. *Journal of Cross-Cultural Psychology, 37*(6), 742-760, doi: 10.1177/0022022106292081.

Cohen, R.J., Swerdlik, M.E., & Sturman, E.D., (2013). *Psychological testing and assessment: An introduction to tests and measurement* (8th ed.). New York, NY: McGraw Hill.

de Anda., D. (1984). Bicultural socialization: Factors affecting the minority experience. *Social Work, 29* (2), 101-107, doi: 10.1093/sw/29.2.101.

Kim, S.Y., Shen, Y., Huang, X., Wang, Y., & Orozco-Lapray, D. (2014). Chinese American parents' acculturation and enculturation, bicultural management difficulty, depressive symptoms, and parenting. *Asian American Journal of Psychology, 5*(4), 298-306. doi: 10.1037/a0035929.

Lesińska, M. (2014). The European backlash against immigration and multiculturalism. *Journal of Sociology, 50*(1), 37-50, doi: 10.1177/1440783314522189.

Lou, E., Lalonde, R.N., & Giguère, B. (2012). Making the decision to move out: Bicultural young adults and the negotiation of cultural demands and family relationships. *Journal of Cross-Cultural Psychology, 43(*5) 663-670, doi: 10.1177/0022022112443414.

Massey, D.S., & Pren, K.A. (2012). Unintended consequences of US immigration policy: Explaining the post-1965 surge from Latin America. *Population and Development Review, 38*(1), 1-29.

Messner, D. (2015, September 11). *A five-point plan for dealing with the refugee crisis: there are no small solutions to big problems*. Retrieved from http://www.die-gdi.de.

Miramontez, D.R., Benet-Martínez, V., & Nguyen, A.M.T.D. (2008). Bicultural identity and self/group personality perceptions. *Self and Identity, 7*, 430-445, doi: 10.1080/15298860701833119.

Mok, A., & Morris, M.W. (2009). Cultural chameleons and iconoclasts: Assimilation and reactance to cultural cues in biculturals' expressed personalities as a function of identity conflict. *Journal of Experimental Social Psychology, 45*, 884-889, doi: doi:10.1016/j.jesp.2009.04.004.

Nguyen, A.M.T.D., & Benet-Martínez, V. (2013). Biculturalism and adjustment: A meta-analysis. *Journal of Cross-Cultural Psychology, 44*(1) 122-159, doi: 10.1177/0022022111435097.

Organisation for Economic Co-operation and Development [OECD].
    (2014). *Is migration good for the economy*. Paris, France: Jean-
    Christophe Dumont & Thomas Liebig.

Pok, B. (2012). Mass Migration. The Wiley-Blackwell Encyclopedia of
    Globalization.

Ruist, J. (2015). The fiscal cost of refugee immigration: The example
    of Sweden. *Population and Development Review, 41*(4), 567-
    581, doi: 10.1111/j.1728-4457.2015.00085.x.

Schain, M.A. (2009). The state strikes back: Immigration policy in the
    European Union. *The European Journal of International Law,
    20*(1), 93-109, doi: 10.1093/ejil/chp001.

Smith, P.B., Fischer, R., Vignoles, V.L., & Bond, M.H. (2013).
    *Understanding social psychology across cultures: Engaging
    with others in a changing world* (2nd ed.). Thousand Oaks, CA:
    Sage Publications.

Verkuyten, M., & Pouliasi, K. (2002). Biculturalism among older
    children: Cultural frame switching, attributions, self-
    identification, and attitudes. *Journal of Cross-Cultural
    Psychology, 33*(6), 596-609, doi: 10.1177/0022022102238271.

Verkuyten, M., & Pouliasi, K. (2006). Biculturalism and group
    identification: The mediating role of identification in cultural
    frame switching. *Journal of Cross-Cultural Psychology, 37*(3),
    312-326, doi: 10.1177/0022022106286926.

Weede, E. (2012). Mass Migration: Cost or Benefit. *Hungarian
    Review, 6*(6). Retrieved from

http://www.hungarianreview.com/article/20151119_mass_immi
gration_cost_or_benefit_.

Weir, P.M. (2011). *U.S. and them: An incremental approach to immigration reform.* Center for the Study of the Presidency and Congress, 1-13.

Xie, Y. (2013, October). *Gender and family in contemporary China* (Report No. 13-808). Retrieved from http://www.psc.isr.umich.edu.

www.ingramcontent.com/pod-product-compliance
Lightning Source LLC
Chambersburg PA
CBHW051901250726
48659CB00006B/2343